crossing the bloodline

angela platt

Published by Leaf by Leaf
an imprint of Cinnamon Press
Meirion House
Tanygrisiau
Blaenau Ffestiniog
Gwynedd, LL41 3SU
www.cinnamonpress.com

ISBN: 978-1-78864-900-1

British Library Cataloguing in Publication Data. A CIP record for this book can be obtained from the British Library.

Designed and typeset in Palatino by Cinnamon Press.

Cover design by Adam Craig © Adam Craig.

Cinnamon Press is represented in the UK by Inpress Ltd and in Wales by the Books Council of Wales.

Acknowledgements

Acknowledgements are due to the editors of the publications where the following poems have appeared: *Crucible* (Orbis vol.160, 2012); *What You Know About Golf* as *Rough Justice* (The Interpreter's House vol.49, 2012); *Night Apart* (Lateral Moves 9, 1995); *The Magic Room* (Reflections 41, 2001).

First Steps, When You Are Ten, Growing Pains, In Absentia, Snapshots and *Grandparents* (Wye Valley Writers' anthology Milestones, Borderlines 8, 2014); *Grace Cup* (Borderlines 10, Heritage, 2018).

I'm indebted to my mentor Jay Whittaker who helped guide me through the collection compiling process, to Wye Valley Writers who gave useful feedback on work in progress and to Newport Stanza poets for their painstaking constructive criticism of my poems.

In addition I'd like to thank my two creative writing groups whose enthusiasm and willingness to try new things fires my imagination to keep on writing. A special thank you is due to my husband Greg for his encouragement and patient listening to first drafts and for valuing my poetry passion.

Contents

For Greg

crossing the bloodline

Kin

She promised you a beach
to swim, and sand.
Discovered only docks.

Southampton special outing,
she and you.
Father T.A. manoeuvring,
Salisbury Plain.

At *The Rose and Crown*
you bedroom tap each wall.
No secret-passage sound.
What next? Drawstring lips.
At last, your first shrill whistle blast.

She finds Southampton baths
for her pent-up ten-year fireball.
Vast blue, all for you.

A fish, you flip and slip,
count how long beneath,
count more until your breath...

the belching engine pump
monster of the deep
might any minute pounce
eat up spit out...

but still you linger
basking in her single-focused gaze.
This once, her only child.

Laughing Gas

At five a galloping horse
he bucks a pan of scalding stew,
his shoulder skin-marbles indelibly.

At eight he climbs the leather chair
masks his face, turns on the tap,
his father's empty dental room
the door agape, to make him laugh.

At ten gutter crouching he points
to a wheel. Biker frog-leg kick-starts
a loud *brrrm brrrm,* spokes spin.
One bloodied index finger sliced in half.

Parents send him off to boarding school
to curb his curiosity,
learn stiff Edwardian silences,
to fit the soldier mould.

Decades on, your father
banishing decorum
docked finger up his nose
to make his children laugh.

Fingers Pressing

Small shoulders draped in classic tulle
ivory skin, blonde curls camera-frame
her fifteen years of brown-eyed symmetry.

Full-grown she hides the dirt
beneath plain sight, allows her children sun
sometimes before the rain.

Shot-silk blouse a touch of class.
Shapely curves in tailored suit,
collar cuffs and toning scarf.

Who's fairest? in her mirror,
knowing that it's her. Slim ankles
are her yardstick to measure others by.

Precision-aimed her quick-tongue lash
turns soughing willow sighing
on sleepy afternoons.

Limelight shuns the wallflower's shade.
Her contours not for child-climbing,
scenic beauty filmed through glass.

Invisible fingers. Sharp nails.
Pressing.

Proclamation

Down four giant steps to kitchen.
In the fireplace the black pram squats.
She rolls across a table the floured pin.
Edging the window, dishes drain

sun shimmers a rusty swing,
four legs lean in chicken-spotted grass,
straight path licks the high stone wall.

Suddenly he's here, door-framed, tall.
Your father in civvies coat lifting his brimmed hat
tames Brylcreemed hair like Moses parting waves.

You turn, look up, stare.

The King is Dead

Four words hang like the swing.
A drawing in of breath. Your mother wipes her fingers
on her apron. Hand to neck she turns the wireless knob.
A crackling hiss: ... *The News.*

The wicked queen with poison in your head.
You picture Snow White's coffin carried through a wood.
And now the king is dead!
You jolt the bitter apple from your throat.

Grandparents

framed in black
in your pram
you lean and peep
arch your back
curl your toe

mother cameo`d
behind scrubbed pine
sprinkles dust
rolls the pin

pastry s p r e a d
g r o w i n g

you do not know it yet

from the door
a dot of light
a sound
pushes   s p r e a d s
eats the space
g r o w s

faces hands noise
tear the room apart
you bawl

grandparents

you do not know it yet

First Steps

Rucked sleeves
cling elephant skin
to plump squat child.

You're propped,
penned by maternal feet.
Cousins chat, sip tea.
Welsh cake crumbs
dot the rug.

You heave your body free,
square shoes pitch out
stomp fibres on two Michelin legs
target the towering china dog.

Chubby embrace, you up it,
teeter back
tilting the room.

Talk stop
breath hold
eyes watch
your tottering
body lurch...

A mini fork-lift truck
straight-arm release
landing the dog
unscathed
on all four feet.

Small nose to painted tongue
one dimpled arm upstretched
patting its shiny head.

Crucible

Too high on the sill
for a tip-toe girl
looking in,
unless you tilt
the large china cup.

Filled to the brim,
apricot plum apple and peach
cornucopia-glazed to the rim.

You imagine a bite of apricot
apple crunch plum suck
drained to the stone,
juice saliva tickling your chin.

The fruit dish rocks
as you turn around,
a shattering crash in your wake.

White-faced looking back
rainbows sun-shaft

a spl i nt er ed   m
                                  o s
                                        a i c
                                                          floor.

Legs sting from the SLAP
your belly a stone,
the bowl for evermore
                                          gone.

Imager of Light

I'm left here to silence
rusting in the rain.

Sun sinking fast, tree shadows
darken. Leaves and grasses fan
cool breeze and darkling motes,
black shapes stirring.

Night creatures may disturb
my hide, dislodge me from
the solid branch you placed me on.

If I should fall, those images
you took such care to make
would shatter ... your running laughing
children sliding dunes at *Merthyr Mawr*.

Footprint hollows shrink, elide.
Soon, as if they'd never been
here at play on this one day.

The leaden sky above me fills
with ragged cloths. Night sounds
unnerve. Children's likenesses
within, though they are curled at home
asleep and may not grow in me.

That long same day, in dark
you've come! How could I doubt?
Carefully you hunt, recall at last
beside which tree you'd stood
freezing the tumbling laughter
with a click.

Fingers inch the knobbled branch
cold metal edge
find leather skin pulled tight,
retrieving my box-shaped frame.
Old friend, my clip fits your finger-stub
as if another limb.

You wipe away my tear,
sling my strap across your marbled shoulder,
march the long miles forward
into memory.

Buddleia

Mid-stride it lurches your gait,
scent-traps you, that straddling limb.
Time shifts *ping!* to scrawny-girl fit
scuffing sandals up two scraggy trunks.

Purple fists poke their fizzy perfume
at a four-eyed wing's long sucking tongue
to the orange-spot butterfly bloom,
a buzz coming close to your ear.

Needle-sharp sting pricks your holding arm
you catapult yawl-bawling down.
Your eyes are agape as the starch bag she tied
turns your skin a washday sky-blue.

Blue starch bags used to whiten and stiffen laundry pre-washing machines were sometimes used for soothing wasp stings.

Taking it Back

She wriggles into, zips part way,
white triangle slit-peeking
from her M&S skirt.

Cut on the bias, spiral swish
she frowns: *Why did I buy it?*
A garment drama brewing.

Curves a little thicker than she'd like,
the mirror offends her eye.
I look like a barrel in this!
I'm taking it back.

It's shortened, but who'd know?
She's proud of her machine-like stitches
delicately spaced, neat knot,
thread snapped between her teeth.

Defiant counter stare-down.
It's too small. You don't have my size.
I want my money back.

Customer service girl inspects the skirt
looks closely at the hem. Open mouth falters
clams shut, catching your mother's eye.

Your size fourteen is skimpy,
they've cheated on the cloth!
M&S meant quality once. Not now!

Bell rings for the manager. Mother primed
on outrage repeat stares seniority down.
A queue is snaking an audience.
Give the lady a voucher. Next...

Heel turn straight back
jaunty chin held high
away she strides.

You have to admire her gall.

Into the Dark

You, your baby brother
straying further than you should.
Crossing a bridge
you spy a hole
below the grassy bank.
Churned tussocks, sand.
No-one around.

Giant pipes just lying.
You scramble down,
find one your size
and in you go.
Loose chalky stones,
hands feel your way
into the dark.

Footsteps sound for miles.
You chase big strides
boom boom,
short steps *tap tap,*
morse code your journey
to the Earth's core.

What if ... they pump in water
seal the pipe? Nobody knows
you're here!

Heart drumming louder than your feet
you fumble on, eclipsed.
Gone too far, no back-tracking now.

Count the steps, you tell him
make them long, to hide you're scared.
A bump, a join, a bend.
Pitch black turns
blotched shadow
shades to grey
to slivered light.

Scalp thump, mouth dry
you search the arc for signs,
willing it to grow.
Shoes scuff, feet lurch,
knees scrape scree.
Your brother cries.

Panting, running, terrified ...

...in your head
you're out and free
in your head
you're up the bank
in your head
you're home.

Flecks of beige
concrete joints
flash past.

Roof-glued tongue
stitch in your hip
shoes crunch stones.

Knees piston on
brain shunts your legs
by-passes the lead between.
Feet up-gear
ratchet leg gallop
push push to bust.

Arms wing-splay
fingers pierce the light...

you shriek
and grab
          the sky.

Grandpa Morgan

Waist string suspends pin-striped trousers
bending for straw to lay for his pigs.
Feeding malt cubes from gnarled working hands
he pats the flank of his favourite mare
whispers sweet nothings in tender male timbre,
large Adam's apple vibrating horse love.

Eye-twinkling mischief serving the ladies
sausage per pound in his own market stall.
Slamming the fridge door, hefting a carcass,
sheep's eyes stare from the grooved wooden block.
Refined fat trembles, embroidered lace swinging,
ceiling-hooked hams hanging salted and stiff.

Blood-soaked pocked shoes polished to iron,
stick legs will-powered by vulcanized knees.
Shin scarred purple from haymaking pitchfork
under the slim-hipped patched suit on his frame.
Fob watch breast-dangles, head shakes disapproving,
tutting *Duw Duw*, a frown on his brow.

Teeth in a glass, pale cheeks curving inwards,
open-mouthed snores through his lightning-rod nose.
Popping sweet wrappers between toothless gums
he splutters, eyes open, three small faces smiling,
swallows his temper discreetly away.
Years on and older, beware if we're bad...

Terror-struck, quaking, will he be telling?
You'll face the music, it's curtains for you!
Woodland, Moor, Stream his favourite read.
Nature's his love apart from the starlings
squabbling for crumbs from Nana's old pinny.
Not worth a light, two a penny he'd say.

At fourteen years old like brothers and parents
his grammar school place relinquished to farm.
A handsome young Horse Guard in sepia photos
he finds no glory in that first world war.
Upright sleeping in stench-laden trenches,
his lips sealed thereafter of battle and death.

Skin wafer-thin still tending his roses,
buttonhole petals adorning best suit.
Balding white head, a tilted ice landing
for free-flying budgies all named *Billie Boy*.
To his gentle coaxing their cobalt wings lifting
droppings like snow, they swoop from the rail.

Shoulder bones shrinking into his nineties
dosed up on malt-flavoured cod liver oil
like malted hay cubes mingling with horse sweat
in hessian sacks he stored in the barn.
A towering colossus was your Grandpa Morgan,
memories spilling, distilling their brew.

Hot Words

In his sick bed your brother swore!
You strain to catch what words,
what joys of flesh in innocence he'd spewed.

Delirious in your parents' room he'd babbled,
tossed and turned in his wheeled-in bed,
sweat beads fevering his brow, cheeks flushed,
ginger coir mat plastering his face.

At cool recovery the mercury dived.
Sisters, hushed, ear wig at the door
hear your brother being punished
for *filthy words* he can't later recall.

Freshly alert, you listen for clues,
a lexicon of smut in playground talk
you hadn't known before.

My Feet Didn't Move!

You diving headlong
over roots of your father,
wherever they're planted
he claims regal stake.

No-one dare touch them,
dimpled white skin,
ten straight dolly pegs
on two perfect feet.

No-one must stray there
heel sole toe holy ground
territory taken
his will not budge.

Spatial awareness
once deemed superior
in males sure to handle
the motor car best

strangely seems absent
in perambulation
moving round people
with his plates of meat.

My Feet didn't move!
the voice of authority
jury and judge...
who dares disapprove?

Cardigan Bay

I

It seeped into your skin;
electricity kindled
you that day.

Knee-high in sea
clear as liquid air
you shoulder-wrapped
the curve.

Scanning the coast
you'd swear
the whole of Wales
was there to see between
your tiny outstretched arms.

II

Blue veins lick knees
with fiery dragon tongues,
hard ground beneath
your feet six decades on
yet still that inner smile
as Atlas arms out-splay.

Map-making god
of all that you survey,
you circumscribe the Bay.

Yellow

Mrs Pitt, drunk as a canary
dressed all in yellow
sidles down Ewenny Road
one high-heeled shoe on pavement
the other in the gutter
lemon hat askew.

You watch her pass,
nose glued to glass.
You must not stare
to see her scary eye.

You like the colour,
buttercups and daffodils,
sun-bright amongst
the green and brown,
the greying town.

But you know saying it
will bring the sister brother taunt:
You'll be like Mrs. Pitt
if you like yellow! yellow! yellow!

So
you crane your neck,
don't look her in the eye
but stare at sky,
and favour blue.

Nicking the Picnic

Grandpa's Austin 7 oozes damp leather,
below small feet, white line tar shine
flickers through rust-holes in the floor.

He turns off the engine, ski-slides the downhills,
restarts the throbbing on the upward slow crawl.

Under the railway arch one more hill glide
onto a bumpy track, dust fills your nose.

Fence-tied hens' claws, beaks dripping red,
bumped in the back seat, tussocky grass
into a thistle field edged by a barn.

Nana spreads newspaper over the prickles
for sisters to eat bread doorstops with jam.

Suddenly a loud crash, a flash and rain-slash
drenching faces and neatly-tied plaits.
Grandpa starts running, opens the barn door

*shoo*s out the pigs, you tumble inside.
Side by side watching the gap-in-wall peepshow
squealing and honking, pigs root in frenzy

chasing wet newsprint, tossing the debris.
Snouts in the feast that was yours.

Hopscotch

Clanging bell. Tumult released
from pent-up rooms.
Chalk nugget in your fist, you're
today's queen bee, scanning yard
for smooth tarmac, palest grey.
Stone cools your small-cupped hand.

Children tail your navy flannel coat.
Tongue from jutted lip, you make your mark,
a streak of white, scuffing knee and toe,
backward beetle crawl setting the trail.

Sudden upward spring, you pace the space,
from knuckled thumb reel a stretch
one knee to ground crabways,
redraw a stripe to meet it headlong
boxing yourself in.

Quick-flash lines slick as taut ropes.
Two more down, you number squares,
step back, admire your handiwork
secreting gold. White tell-tale powder
stains your pocket-slit.

Drones hang back, await the call.
Hand on hip spreading your girth,
you turn to face the throng,
finger-point, name one-by-one
game players.

Team complete,
rejected classmates pout their lips
scatter buzz-bluster
brawl punch and sting.

Under the Skin

I

Anaesthetised by alcohol and fags
piano-playing sing-song nights,
their *Hollybush* homeward jaunt
ended with a bang.

Landed nose- first from pony and trap
...a wonder she wasn't killed.
Mum's washed and spun half-truth...

Moonlit curtains flicked. Outside
their pebble-dashed semi,
Grandpa's horse buck-twisted,
threw the cart askew.

Nana, airborne, scribed an arc,
face down landed in grit.
She laughed in her mirror
... carrying on!

Powdered pumice centre-piece
adorned her florid cheeks.
Nan's fruit bowl's scab-picked oranges,
peeled zest masking nicotine,

II

Upstairs dusting mid-collapse
she waved her yellow duster into space,
a fireball in her brain.

A passer-by caught her signal,
through open window heard the thud.

Rippled adult frowns admonish: *hush!*
to uttered innocence: *is she dead?*

III

Holding your mother's hand you stare.
Gold letters wink from a marble slab.

A place where sparks make smoke
and then she's gone.

Nana laughing, waving.
                    Her yellow duster   fading.

When You Are Ten

A black cat bobs through swampy grass. Blackbird squawk alert, sleek predator hones in for the kill, pounce-dives at the nest-fallen bald grey mite cradled in wet green. Peering through glass your heart thumps to overdrive racing your legs outdoors. You shoo the feline, straddle the yellow beak's slow breath, one tiny eye-closed pulse. Foot certain heel hammers the ground, stamping out its pain.

Dull *thud thud* mat shoe-scrape, entrails sweat through nightly dreams, haunt your day-pale eyes in pouring rain.

*

That same year climbing the long hill home, satchel on your back. Unleashed on the pavement ahead of you the brown dog leaps the road, the car steam-rollers down.

Pulped belly, four bent legs stick-point at sky, death-throe howls tearing at your ears.

Silence.

That freeze-framed second when you know you'd give your life to save that dog.

You'll never feel this much again.

*

Porthmadog

Boxed houses cling
to the slope of a hill

Sun crackles heat
salt parching the air

Beak-shrieking gulls
peck harbour-grey stones

Tang of pailed crabs
sidle, dip-dive

Babble of voices
slowly unreels

the spool of this child,
that saint-patient girl

looping a line
dangling pink feet

on the brick salty wall
hoping for starfish

sea spray in your hair
skin sunburn-tingling

in dreams you are there

Innocence

Those men, spiked beards
gnarl-knuckled knocks on Nana's door
calling their sibilant spits, *ed!*
screeched high end-note: *en*
Knives, blades, shears, scissors sharp

Carborundum wheel on a cart, large as a roller
to flatten grass. Grit ring, grey gravel
rice-pud currants, spotted dick set hard

in stone. Wide-eyed you watch
steel glinting in the sun, orange
flecks of fireworks fly,

broad-daylight Catherine wheel
spinning its high-pitched whine.
Jamming fingers in your ears,
you feel a warm wind blowing.

Mind now, she shouts,
head bent over mangle, guiding
pancaked overalls into a bucket.

Don't get in his way
she means.
No thought back then
of strangers' blades that pierce,
tear flesh,   spill blood.

Garden Party

Coloured dots on rippling towels
catapult you...
...to spots in fizzy orangeade,
three glasses, matching jug,
red yellow blue and green,
a table cloth, rippling.
Auntie Mary's lips chirp cheery words,
chocolate-button eyes smile down. You,
at four, holding an open book.
You're dumbstruck shy. Every birthday
her book's arrival anchors you.

Straight path in chicken-spotted grass.
Down the high wall loops a green caterpillar,
ripple-pattern eyes along his back.
You nest him snug in a Hornby train,
feed him grass and leaves and love.
He grows, performs his magic trick and
vanishes. You look and look and look
wet-eyed, tin carriage rusting in the rain.

Steroid-swollen cheeks, dulled eyes,
black spot ingressing Auntie Mary's brain.
The hope she gifted you deserts her now.
Her tumour grows. She sheds her skin
and vanishes.

Cruel trick.

Had she tried preparing you?
That last gift: *Three at Cherry-Go-Gay*
a treasure hunt, no treasure found.
First disappointing read,
missing a foothold on the path.

You see her smiling now, her timbre
like rustling pages turning in the wind.

Grace Cup

From the shiny full-cheeked teapot
you pour an arc of twisted glass,
ginger flavouring the citrus cup.

Sipping infusion from the rim
you glance at the pot
in cold white day.

A face looks back at you,
contoured crevices enlarged;
red veins, no youthful blush.

Mis-
match.

In your head
your younger self

no longer there.

Particles
have reconfigured.

Blissful, you'd been unaware.

A moment present

dis- con
nects
from past.

Cast
adrift

until
inside
your brain

a face you recognise

catches up again.

Grown Woman Hiding

Blue-green-grey speck of miracle
pin-point lens to view the world
innocent and small
coyly peeps at camera.

In the photograph
an elephantine mass,
capacious legs and arms
shoulders, thighs
space-grab
that nonchalant lean.

Where is the speck of light
within, coy, small, thin?

What came between?

The Magic Room

Red leather stool clothes-polished smooth,
you finger brass buttons Brailling the rim
watching the chimney smoke curl and unfurl
like Nana's coiled hair, fading and grey.
Creatures and castles shape-shift in coal
in the cradle-black basket holding the fire.
Maroon chenille fringes oak table leg,
diamond-light patterned from window-lead panes.

Yeast fragrance filters through stretched muslin cloth,
Nana's mixing bowl placed in the hearth.
Melodies climb gently fall and slow fade,
shadows dancing on sideboard and wall.

Her outstretched arms languor on dimpled elbow
harmonies trickle, her fingers trapeze
the black and cream notes in cushioning gums
nestling like teeth to a final plié.

Shutting piano lid clicking the lock.
It's time to get tea, she snaps on the light.
Enchantment vanished the spell has been cast.
One proven seed planted in you.

Paroxysm

He leans over the pulpit
as if to leap,
fanned arms, attacking.
Fire and brimstone ricochet
round the cavernous cage
boom vitriol, escalates
decibelled passioned wrath.

Stiff-boarded congregation
earth-pewed as cabbages
in rooted rows avert their gaze.

You dare not look at him,
stare ahead at pinioned eagle wings,
brass feathered ormolu
holding the giant lectern down.

Bubbling up from throats
the giggles come. Shoulders shake,
faces blush, biting tongues,
gagging mouths with handkerchiefs,
the ripples from one girl to next
along the choir front pew
rivering exploding mirth.

            Finger-waving rage
pours down on you ...

You girls should be ashamed!
This is God's house!

We bow our heads,
await the quaking ground
the tumbling pillars
cracking walls ...

He moderates to drone.

Displacement

Where did ego hide
when two young boys
told you to jump
far out from that vertical
funfair slide?

Innocent of
devilish intent,
the id in you just leapt.

Cartoon capers
off a cliff, your body
stayed mid-air

till ego grasped
at gravity

and down you went.

Growing Pains

She dither-flaps
at your bed end,
nearing your bundled clothes
on the corner chair.

Sharp against the light
white knickers
stained brown-red
waved mid-air.
I knew it!
Why didn't you tell me?

Shocked mute
your heart hammers
anvil on iron ...
you hadn't known.

Get up now...
your sister'll show you what to do.
When you've finished
mind you wash down below.

Filtering grey
the net curtain reclaims the room.
Action replays in your head.
Cool breezes slow your heart.
You are a woman now.

But when you have finished,
why must you wash your feet?

Five Floors High

You're here to say goodbye.

She comes, this harbinger in uniform,
warm vowels like cups of tea.
She slipped peacefully away...
as if the altitude had helped her passing,
as if her battle now could be erased.

Amoeba streaks on hospital glass.
When someone dies it rains.
Winds beat the seagull cries to silence.

You, unknowing, sipped coffee
in the basement, read a poem.
A transcendental blip,
her rattling rasps had ceased.

That same nurse hovering on guard, you bend,
kiss your mother's cavernous grey,
face shadowing the next sea change.

Five flights of stairs
before your feet have touched the ground.
Before the numb umbilical ache.

Nana

Someone's here to speak to you,
the medium trawls you in.
She says you're high up on a swing
showing you can fly.

Piano fingers cascade
glissando- tripping dainty notes
flamed pictures in the coal,
shadows flickering the hearth.

Reciting words her rhymes unfold:
A little girl sits under a tree
sewing at twilight, straining to see
silhouette geese sky-forming a V.

Her bedtime games would terrify:
Here comes the bogey man, quick run!
Inside her book of country verse
a spider lurks long after she's gone.

Struggling to remove your boot
you hard-kicked her leaded door.
From three years old the hole remained,
your eternal shame.

Grandpa's lap, you smell the sea,
salted hams on ceiling hooks.
He's humming songs and lullabies
while Nana mends his socks.

Ample bosom, apron tied
Nana unzips the knobbly pods,
shelling peas in a colander,
you catch them as they drop.

She speaks to you of early days,
world-easy days and daisy chains
when you were young
and you had wings to fly.

Hockey

Jolly hockey sticks! posh people sometimes say
but mention of that *h* word will not jolly you.
Less than sportsmanlike, you have no wish to play
that so-called game where favourite girl, *get her!*

stands centre pitch, stick and ball to bully-off,
her pawns mere satellites placed willy-nilly round
the field. As for this left-handed, scoffed-at waif,
right-handed useless hockey stick, drowned by rain

beneath bruised clouds, goose-pimpled on the edge
pretending you're involved, can't even *see* the ball.
Will someone notice slinking off behind the hedge?
You're supernumerary. Barely here at all.

What You Know about Golf

Just that once at Wenvoe
your left handed ladies' club
catapulted the hard white
pitted sphere high into the air
a mile or more.

It landed in the rough
where placid sheep cocked eyes
but went on chewing evening mist.

Perhaps they knew the pristine ring
that caught the setting sun
in its reflection
like wet-grass diamonds
in early morning dew

would mark your finger out
for harder things
than playing games

Snapshots

I

He and you
mismatched
tidily framed
looking out.

II

You've shaken
inertia
from your hair,
split ends
outgrow the mount.

III

Unframed
Wild child
Alive.

Sacrificial Lamb

Your mother:
No children at the wedding,
they'll spoil the day.

So now your friends can't come.
But who are you to say?
Stitched up between
this older man with love,
he says, enough for two
and her maternal rule.

One day you'll feel the same.
He's self-assured, exudes complacency.
At nineteen you just want it over,
to leave. No going back.

Tucked in bed that final time
she tip-toes in and kisses you.
Did she ever place her lips
upon your skin?
You can't recall,
can't believe she would.

Mumbling *goodnight*
through burning cheeks,
you practise saying: *I do.*

Candy stripes against bedroom glass,
the iron sits on the ironing board
waiting to press your gown
as dawn light filters through.
Your keep-safe barrier from mishap,
abduction by the dog with saucer eyes
or any change of plan.

Kissing The Blarney Stone

Drenched honeymooners
upward trek to Blarney Castle,
thinking the stone firmly rooted in earth.
Hooded figures, plastic macs aswish,
doused by April dollops of Irish rain.

High on the castle wall
a slab of stone,
looking for all the world
like a slab of stone.

The full smacker
would need some welly
like the sensible footwear
you should have worn
for the castle climb.

Trapeze artist's grip,
hands welded to wet rail
you limbo flip , no guide to hold
your arching back, mouth pouts
the bussing rock,
lips cushioning cold slime.

Gift of the gab
you already had.
The Blarney Stone
gifts you instead
a curdling acerbic tongue.

Off-Loading

Duplicate toasters rugs cracked old mugs chairs table
piled on a trailer in pouring rain.
You join queueing cars arcing a muddy field
waiting to feed junk to the skip,
bask in the warm sealed bubble of his car.

You wellington step into the squelch,
beckon him nearer to off-load.
His trailer tyre plants your toes in the mud.
You try to walk, wobble, fall back in a puddle.

From the circus ring of cars you hear guffaws.
They see you centre stage,
a clown in baggy pants writhing in slime.
His head turns, chuckling.
That's when you laugh too,
wallow in the oozing of your love.

Ice Cream Dreams

After Wendy Cope

Pavlovian pleasure, the van's tinkling bell,
your mouth's overflowing with drips.
The thought of creamy-cool taste on your tongue
you salivate, moist shiny lips.

The weather is close, and so is your love,
sun peeps through a cloud stretching thin.
A gust swipes two cones from his hands to the ground.
You laugh at the typical him.

Past Tense

Evening greys to dusk. You turn your key.
Ashtray dottle, pipe cleaner bent black,
ghost-rings in saucepan, egg shell
on draining board, painkiller foil
crushed in a silver ball.
Ash on the floor like grey hair
unravelling.

He's gone.
The still, sad air rewinds.

Mid-morning he shuts your door,
alone at eighty three,
her brown-eyed smile, her missing scent
and shampooed hair
permeates his wafer skin.

Earlier as you left for work
he, bleary-eyed in dressing gown
hugging you goodbye.

His arms
too tight
too long
holding you...

her replica.

Leitmotif

Ascendant piano notes trickle like stars
up the stairs. Nana's upright piano
painted dusky pink.
She would have laughed.
Children's songs, he's carolling a hymn
in apple leaves, curved fruiting blush,
the silver highs and gentle chords of bass
lifting the world's expansive heart.

Lingering grip, ice damp begins to edge
invisibly away. Dull yesterday
folds up its blanket self, unpeeling cold,
dissolving calloused skin.
A warmer kissing breath outside the glass,
birds' chattering pitch rises a notch.

A sudden flutter.
Flag-waving leaves turn instantly as one,
heliotroping the brightest star,
trooping to the colour of the sun.

Six Five Two Nine Two

A singing in her breath,
a reaching out expectantly
until the words that follow
curtail the mesmerising chant:
Six five two nine two ...

I hear her linger
on a sigh, so part of her,
stretched vowel cadences
riding her humpbacked tongue.

On that final utterance
she hears your voice,
a wave sweeps in
and something dies.

Whoever she had thought
might call,
you don't hide your surprise...

...it wasn't you.

In Absentia

She was the last you'd tell
of hurt, of feeling low
or upbeat, a new dress
the last to show,
a poem published
or a hard-won prize;
you'd tried for long enough
to catch her eyes.

Yet now you find yourself
turning
toward the shelf
to telephone.
Her number plays inside your head
but she is gone.

Night Apart

Trains pummel the ground
punctuate the night
slicing the air.
Cocooned in your dressing gown
an extra skin
you trace your body curve
stroke your hair
cup your left breast
turn to the wall.
Your stomach
gurgles in monologue
missing his snores.

Remnant

Putting on her fabric-weakened
bobbled last remaining piece
bruising easily

this blouse is irreplaceable,
its delicate survival
one last thread of her,
matching skirt long gone.

Laundered, cool,
no lingering armpit smell of her
as after snow she folded you
in turn to her, warmed
unmittened hands
in her moist armpit hollows
till the painful throbbing ceased.

Close to the beating of her heart.

Looking Glass

Her bevelled oblong mirror
chestnut frames two closed doors
on your half landing.
The third stands open, light splaying
a picture gallery at gable end.

Staggered photographs,
offspring in robes
with graduation scrolls,
parents coupled against
a faded ivy-covered shed
littering the sun-lit wall.

Her frozen smile,
a mother's knowing eyes
pitted against the day.
At camera flash
her future pinned.

Looking in her mirror then
did she sense she'd be
forever posing on his arm?

Paper House

Layered spittle
from a thousand mouths
delicate and strong
suspended from a beam.

Pre-dawn you wake,
raw nerve holding.
Out of your mouth accretions
form a shape you hardly recognise.

Stale taste of compromise
sours your tongue. The wasps,
emerging, sting. He reels...

spits barbs back at you.
Alliance negated in a single spat.
Your house of cards collapsing.

Walking Hot Coals

A large wood pigeon mute on a bough
unnerved by profusion of song.
All winter long he's reigned,
coo-calling in an indifferent air.
Now he's well-behaved
allowing small birds voice.

For days you've harboured his silences
crooked them in your arms
like bundles of wilting snowdrops
till shades of evening whisper.

One-sided tempered words
replay. The bubbling cauldron calms.
Your fingers play old hurts, trawl burnt
remains, tease-fray charred pages,
holding blackness at bay.

Coming out, he sees you freeze,
breaks silence he claims he doesn't own.
You crash in on him, accuse.
He blanches, eyes shock-wide.
Words walk hot coals, leap on contact,
ignite the spark.

Gravity of different planets
tugs and reels
light years distancing.

Talking in Clogs

I'd better water the plants.
He stretches, yawns a lion's cave,
sun already high ignoring him
as he ignored its path.

Your lizard tongue
veers a dangerous zig zag,
consonants spit-ricochet
vertiginous vowels.
I think you should do the tiling first.

Clouds suck the sky
vacuum pack the air
language stripped from throats.

Plants shrivel
tiles untouched
an elephant stalks
room to room to room.

You hardly dare breathe
around him.

Decibels of silence
march like clogs on cobbled stones.

The Rumour of Yesterday

Stiff lavender stalks
scagging a sleeve,
pods tied up in muslin,
leg-heavy bees.
Tarred tobacco dottle
tap-scratches a tune,
cake crumbs on cotton
smoke threading yarn.

Red wine bleeding orange
sweats saffron, lipstick streaks
a musky perfume.
Sheet mingling effusions
entwining like thighs.

Payback time.

The story leaks.
An afterword
in a bundled armful
of clothes.

Runaway

Through snow the small removal van
manoeuvres the slush-piled lane.
The men know where you've come from,
what you've left behind.

Entrails of a life. Sofa bed, piano,
hand-made table cradled in.
Turning the van around, the driver waves...
When you change your mind love,
give us a call!

Old fashioned furniture,
soot-black bricks, the fireplace gapes,
your breath ghosts each cold room.
Alcove mirrors throw back red eyes
dishevelled hair, pale skin.
A person you don't recognise.

Hands numb, you shovel coal into the hod,
let out the sobs to metal scrapes on stone.
An old man's shadow, stranger
in the yard is watching you.

Low sun crimsons iced snow,
wool-grey sheep move closer
to the hedge, peer in
at stranded you, corralled.

Calor gas, lined-up torpedoes
stand sentinel against the porch.
Twin tub like your mother's first,
gas hob rings. You spark a flame.
The kitchen walls weep.

Maths

Subtract the love.
Divide. Unravel the solemn vow.

One unit marks the hollow place
once thought eternity.

Quantify the shattered parts
no longer true.

Attempt the equation
asymmetrically.

Summarize the axiom:
zero is not the solution.

Recalculate.
Chart a new topography

like inchworm measures length
and spider weaves its broken web.

Be brave.
Hold fast the particles of you.

Don't let force and distance
make your body fall.

Gravity is weak
but you are strong.

On Meeting The Younger, Wiser You.

After Helen Dunmore

I find you on a swing
striving to dive upward into blue ...
it's there for you.
Your small smooth fleshy hands
clasped tight around the chain
do not resemble these blue veins
bursting above their sacs,
rivers on phalangeal bone,
whirlpool in between.

There you go, letting drop
the rattling chains, seat left swinging
to wander free a riverbank,
a wood, a tunnelled path
looking for the little people,
stepping carefully for fear
they're hiding in a blade of grass,
a door into a tree. If only you could
Alice-shrink, they'd show themselves
to you.

You're growing now to meet
my diminishing.
Level soon, eye-to-eye ...
that sparkle in yours glazing mine.

For the meantime
go and play the long day,
roll in grass, run and leap
and fly that swing high.

Hold on to your dreams.
Keep safe our keepsakes.
For you.
          For me.

Gift

Shrunken knot tight in your chest
resists the pain, closes it firm
stopping the leak. You step on splintered glass
barefoot in your chain mail skin.

Unflinching, you walk. Memory
plays through dreams, shadows your days.
Thoughts gnaw the cocoon, pierce rice paper
in your frail house, crack the windows of your eyes.

Yet even now in a jar on a high shelf
you preserve it, polish and dust
its shell, hold it to the light.
You bequeath your sons this legacy.
This is your gift. Your inner skin. Intact.